Learn to

Discern

According to Scripture

Leslie Allebach
(with Dean Good)

Paperback ISBN: 979-8-9872064-3-0
eBook ISBN: 979-8-9872064-2-3

TABLE OF CONTENTS

Introduction

I believe Jude 3-4 gives us the perfect wisdom as we search for truth and light in the midst of the evil and dark days in which we find ourselves living–

Beloved, while I was very diligent to write to you concerning our common salvation, I found it necessary to write to you exhorting you to contend earnestly for the faith which was once for all delivered to the saints. For certain men have crept in unnoticed, who long ago were marked out for this condemnation, ungodly men, who turn the grace of our God into lewdness and deny the only Lord God and our Lord Jesus Christ.

We are to contend for the faith. As ungodly men twist and pervert the Gospel we are to <u>contend</u>. This is a word that implies strong feeling and action. Synonyms include assert, claim, argue, insist, declare, and profess. How opposite this word *contend* is to words like *ignore* and *overlook*. And how opposite this is, too, to the compromise we see almost daily now in ministries of trusted pastors and authors, who concede key doctrines in the name of unity. Oh, this is not what the Bible teaches us to do! May we remember that–

A warped, perverted gospel is no gospel at all!

I hope you will find this little book a blessing to you as you seek to discern amidst the plethora of speakers, books, and entertainment that claim to represent Christ. May we keep fighting boldly and bravely–always relying on God's Word as our anchor and for our answers!

Below you will find a bit about each chapter. These descriptions will help you if you want to use this book for reference after you have read it through.

Before We Can Learn to Discern--There are some prerequisites for biblical discernment. It is important to have these in place before you begin your journey.

Why Do So Few Seem to Care?—This chapter takes a look at why so few Christians are interested in discernment.

Preparing Your Heart and Mind--Six things we need to BE (or at least be working on) before we can effectively discern. Are these a part of your life?

What Is Biblical Christianity?—This chapter is written by Pastor Dean Good (my brother) on what Christianity is according to scripture. There is so much nonsense that is attributed to God these days, so this chapter will help us set a solid foundation of what Christianity is according to God as written in His Word.

The Corruption of Christianity--This chapter is also written by Pastor Dean. Here he shows six ways that Christianity has been corrupted. While these six things have always existed in one form or another since the inception of Christianity, they are all now working together to bring the church into the coming one-world religion. Read this to find out what, in a nutshell, you should be looking out for.

What Is Your Paradigm?--Before we can do any discerning at all, we have to determine what we are going to use as our barometer for truth. This post looks at this question in light of the Word of God. As Christians, this is our gold standard and becomes the basis for how we view both the world and the church.

Philosophies in Opposition--In this chapter, ten specific philosophies, embraced by mainstream Christianity, are evaluated in light of scripture. This is not an exhaustive list but merely a short list to encourage you to recognize these key false teachings, as well as to encourage you to begin evaluations such as these on your own.

Acknowledging the War--It is impossible to discern if we do not acknowledge the war that is raging in the supernatural world. Scripture makes it clear that Satan is our enemy. Learn why it is critical that we understand this before we can discern properly.

How Do You Determine What Is True, Right, and Good?--Does the fact that something is helpful make it true or right or good? Read this to find out how pragmatism has invaded the church and how this deadly philosophy is changing the method that Christians use to determine truth.

Who Do You Follow?--A curious phenomenon that has been taking place over the past 25-30 years is the obsession with celebrity. We often sacrifice our loyalty to the Word of God for the loyalty to a man (or woman). Read here to find out why this is a big problem and what we can do to make sure we personally do not fall for this trick of Satan's.

Reawakening the Conscience--Does worldly entertainment affect our ability to discern? This post explores this question, while also providing testimonies that back up its premise.

Living in the Light--Discernment is a lonely, discouraging, and unpopular road to take. As we become more and more aware of the darkness around us (particularly in relation to the darkness that has infiltrated the church) we can begin to feel hopeless and sad about the future for both ourselves and for our families. In this chapter we will look to God's Word for encouragement as we learn to discern.

Knowing When to Speak Up--How do we know when something is worth the confrontation? Here are a few guidelines that will help.

How Do I Share What I Am Learning?--Some guiding principles that we should consider as we talk with others about discernment.

When You Need a Little Help—Sometimes we need to do some research. In this chapter you will find some helpful tips and words of caution.

May God bless you as you seek to know the truth in God's Word. The book of Jude ends with these wonderful verses. May they be an encouragement to you as you learn and grow–

Now to Him who is able to keep you from stumbling,
And to present you faultless
Before the presence of His glory with exceeding joy,

To God our Savior, Who alone is wise, Be glory and
majesty, Dominion and power, Both now and forever.
Amen.

Jude 24-25

Before We Can Learn to Discern

It is quite the challenge these days to keep with the plethora of false teachers and the deluge of false teaching that are flowing into the church. It used to be fairly subtle but now it's an all-out war on biblical, historical Christianity. Personally, I find it incredibly discouraging. Never in a million years did I see this coming.

People will sometimes ask me about a specific teacher and I am happy to do a little research and see what I can find out. It usually isn't too hard to figure out if you know what you are looking for.

So how can we know what to look for? Who am I to tell you? Who is anybody to tell you?

This has become a very real issue in this world of strong opinions. On what opinion do you stand? And why do you stand there?

There's really only one way to know and that is through complete and utter reliance on the Word of

God and what it teaches. Before we can learn to discern–and as we are learning to discern–we must spend consistent, daily time in the Word, approaching it with humble submission and a spirit of obedience.

When we do this and when we take the Bible at face-value (*literally*) from beginning to end we will find it *makes so much sense.* Especially in light of what we are experiencing these days.

The Bible predicts a one-world religion. We are watching all religions–including Christianity–being funneled into a global religion even as I write this. This shouldn't surprise us. God told us it would happen (Revelation 17:1-18). This understanding gives us a framework, doesn't it? Whether it happens tomorrow or in a hundred years, we understand Satan's game plan. We know what he is working towards.

We also find out in our Bibles that justification is by faith in Christ *alone* (Romans 10:9-10 and many, many other places). This means that any religion–no matter how "Christian" it sounds–is a false religion if it requires any works as part of salvation. We know that any religion is false if it takes the focus off of the finished work of Christ on the cross.

We find out in God's Word that He condemns drunkenness, sorcery, homosexuality, rebellion, impurity, dissensions, fits of anger, impurity, obscene language (Galatians 5:19-21; Colossians 3:5-9). Knowing this helps us intelligently discern in the world of entertainment and in living our daily lives.

We not only realize that entertainment that incorporates these things should not be a regular part of the Christian's life, but we also know that anyone or any organization that promotes these things is not the real deal. I'm not judging motive or eternal destiny here. People get confused. We are not to judge salvation. But what we can know is that they are *off biblically* and we shouldn't follow them.

These are only three examples that show us how the Bible helps us to discern. You see, it is impossible to keep up with all the false teachers that are out there. But if we are studying our Bibles with the right heart, we will be amazed at how God will open our eyes to what is going on. We will become more aware the more we study the Word.

So what about the people who seem to study the Bible all the time and don't discern at all? This has been a conundrum I have faced for a long time. How does that work?

There are so many things that can keep us from really seeing the truths of scripture, no matter how much we read it. Let's take a look at just three—

1. A proud heart. Many people approach the Word with their preconceived ideas of what they *want* it to say, what they *wish* it would say or what they *think* it should say. God will not give insight to the person who studies the Bible with preconceived notions. We have to humble ourselves and yield ourselves to Him and

His message. How arrogant of us to think we know better than He does! But how easily we can all fall into this trap.

2. A fearful heart. I believe another very real issue is that the ramifications of really believing what the Bible teaches is frightening. The way is narrow? My husband…daughter…mom & dad…are not saved and that means…? It is not a pleasant message. (But, as we all know, pleasantness is irrelevant when it comes to truth. Many people face the Bible's message in a very different way than they would ever face an unpleasant medical diagnosis. Can you imagine ignoring a deadly disease and pretending it's just not there??)

3. A heart that loves sin. This is probably the biggest thing that hinders believers in their biblical discernment. We Christians love our sin. And reading the Bible with a heart to obey means we are willing to give up our sin. But many are just not willing to do this. Whether it's sexual immorality, sorcery, occasional drunkenness, ungodly entertainment, an unforgiving heart–whatever it may be–many of us hold on to these things for dear life, believing (mistakenly) that we can't possibly be happy without them.

———

Do you have any of these attitudes as you approach the scripture? I know I certainly have had them and still do at times. This isn't a "once and done" issue. We must be consistently and intentionally examining our hearts and minds (2 Corinthians 13:5) to make sure we are not becoming hardened through sinful habits or our love for this world.

Recognizing that scripture is our final authority and our only legitimate way to know who God is and what His plan is for mankind will be the first healthy step in learning to discern. God will teach us through His Word if we but take the time to study it with a submissive heart that is willing to obey what it says.

Why Do So Few Seem to Care?

I have found myself wondering recently what my grandmother would think of the church if she were still alive. She went to heaven in 1990, two weeks before my oldest daughter was born. Oh, how the world and, more importantly, the church has changed since that time.

Like the proverbial frog in the pot, I don't think we truly realize how much has changed in those years. But what if she could come back for just a day? How clear would the changes be to her?

I guess it is rather like when we haven't seen a child for a few years. To those who are living with the child, the changes are so subtle and imperceptible that they are hardly noticed. But to someone who hasn't been with the child, the changes are radical.

I believe that this is exactly what is happening now. The changes to the church have been profound and inconceivable and yet so gradual and subtle that many have missed it.

Why have so many people missed these cataclysmic changes? Perhaps it is primarily because of these four reasons—

1. We don't know the Word of God. Biblical illiteracy abounds in those who would profess Christianity today. So few who profess Christ study the Word but are, rather, content to read what someone has to say or write *about* the Word. But if we aren't in the Bible for ourselves, how do we know that we can trust the one communicating what is written there? How can we discern if we don't have a standard by which to judge what we hear?

2. We are distracted and apathetic. Our disinterest in discernment may stem from our lifestyle and wrong priorities. We are busy with other-- and seemingly more important-- things. Things like jobs, education, the arts, sports, church, family, health and fitness, hobbies, and vacations are just a few distractions that draw us away from God's Word. Of course, these things, in and of themselves, are not bad things. But when we allow them to consume all of our passion, time, and enthusiasm it will often leave us too drained and exhausted to be concerned with God's Word and what it says. (How do we fix this? There is an easy solution! Time spent in God's Word, diligently studying it, eliminates apathy towards the truth.)

3. We have been brainwashed to believe that truth is not absolute. Even those of us who call ourselves Christians will fall for this if we aren't careful. I have heard Christians say things like this: *"That book was such a comfort to me, how could it possibly be wrong?"* and *"This book really helped me understand who God is"*–even though the books in question were blatantly and clearly against what scripture teaches. Another phrase we sometimes hear: *"How can you argue against so-and-so's experience?"* regarding someone's account that was in direct opposition to the Word of God. We have allowed truth to be defined by our subjective experiences instead of by the Word of God.

4. And, finally, we are unwilling to pay the cost. The way of discernment is often lonely and hard. It can, and often is, a way filled with ridicule and mockery. If we aren't careful, we will talk ourselves into believing that false teaching or ungodly entertainment doesn't *really* matter, in order to protect ourselves from being ridiculed and rejected.

But are these excuses good enough? Will they stand up when we stand in front of our Holy God and give an account of our lives? Or will we one day deeply regret just how deceived we were? And will we grieve how we, steeped in deception ourselves, unknowingly aided in the deception of others?

Sadly, the choice to discern can come with some heartache and it may cost us in ways that hurt. This means we have some important choices before us: Do we want to follow God or do we want to be popular? (The two are generally mutually exclusive.) Do we want to follow God or do we want to have our ears tickled? And do we want to follow our perfect God or are we going to follow imperfect man? These are serious choices that will have great impact on your life and the lives of those you touch.

I have a great passion for the truth that was passed on to me by my father. He instilled this love for truth in the hearts of both my brother (Pastor Dean Good, co-author of this book) and myself and, in many ways, the ministries that we both have are part of his legacy.

It is my hope that this short book will help you grow in your knowledge of the Word and in your love for the Truth. I hope it will you give you some insight into what is going on in the church (and the world) today and that you will come to understand the critical importance of comparing all you come across to what scripture says.

You may be asking: *What exactly is discernment?* We hear this word, but perhaps you aren't quite sure what it is. In its simplest definition, discernment is the ability to identify truth from error, right from wrong.

It is my hope that this series will help you discern by teaching you how to run any new philosophies, trends, and methods through the grid of scripture. I also hope that it will encourage your loyalty to God and His Word to grow while your loyalty to fallible man–whether they be preachers, authors, musicians, or friends– will be subjected to the Word of God, first and foremost.

Please note, chapters four and five are written by my brother (Pastor Dean Good, mentioned above), who will first give us a definition of biblical Christianity according to the Word of God and, second, give us an overview of how this definition has been warped and twisted and perverted in what we call "Christianity" today. From that foundation, I will then try to give you practical ways to help you as you seek to "learn to discern" for yourself.

A few things to keep in mind as we begin this series–

1. We are *all* called to discern. Sometimes I will hear someone say something like this–"I can't see all that stuff you are talking about. You just have the gift of discernment." There might be some truth to that, but I believe the Bible teaches that all of us–by diligently studying the Word and training our minds to compare all we hear and see with what the Word says–can (and should) become effective discerners. Let's think of this in light of witnessing. Not having the gift of evangelism does not give us the right to ignore the opportunities we get to share the Gospel. All people are called to share the Gospel. It may be a little easier for those who are gifted but it is something we all are called to do. The same principle applies to discernment (Hebrews 5:14; Philippians 1:9-11).

2. The only thing that matters at the end of the day is the Word of God. It matters not what I think *at all*. If you have followed my blog at *Growing4Life* for even a short time, you will already know this but let me say it again– my opinion <u>does not matter</u>. I don't want you to rely on me for truth. Or on Pastor Dean. Or even on your own pastor. Or favorite author or speaker. While we are certainly able to learn and grow from the teachings of other men and women, our job is to search out what the scriptures say for ourselves, running everything *anybody* says through the grid of the Word of God (Acts 17:11). As believers, we must hold to the inspiration, inerrancy, and sufficiency of scripture. Each topic in this series will be studied in light of the Word as it has been traditionally interpreted since it was first written (2 Thessalonians 2:14-15).

3. Discernment is not popular. I touched on this already but I want to reiterate here: As you learn and your eyes are opened, you may be excited to share what you are learning. Please be aware that many people will roll their eyes, change the subject, call you things like *harsh*, *unloving*, or *hyper-critical*, and/or talk about you behind your back. Some will even grow angry with you. Walls may go up between you and friends whom you love. Just as trying to swim upstream feels impossible, so, too, does going against the flow of the mainstream church. Most people are very comfortable swimming downstream and the fact that you are swimming in the opposite direction—no matter if it is based clearly on scripture or not—makes most Christians extremely uncomfortable. Prepare yourself for this and endeavor to always be loving, kind, and gentle as God gives you opportunity to discuss the things you are learning. And never forget that it is that it is the Holy Spirit who opens eyes. Remembering this helps us to stay calm and to back away without rancor when someone just *can't or won't see.* None of this is worth a heated argument. It just isn't. Walk away and pray for them. That's the best thing we can do.

4. We can never judge someone's relationship with God. As I give you examples of men and women who may have fallen for some of these false doctrines and philosophies, the inevitable, panicked questions will be —*Do they know what they are doing? Does that mean they aren't saved?* I want to just say right now <u>that only God knows</u>. There is really no way to know if they have been deceived or if they are purposely deceiving. Only God knows the heart of a man (Jeremiah 20:12). My goal is to show how these philosophies have infiltrated the ministries of those in mainstream Christianity, as well as even many of those that are associated with conservative Christianity. We are unable to, and should not, judge hearts, motives, or eternal destinies. Please keep this in mind.

5. What you do with this information is up to you. Some of you will read this book and grab hold of it and determine to not read or listen to anything by anyone who you know has compromised. Others of you will try to walk the fine line of sorting through the good and the bad as you continue to do the Bible Studies or listen to the sermons of those who are teaching false doctrines. I cannot tell you what to do, but I can tell you what I do. When I become aware that someone is teaching false doctrine, I eliminate them from having any input into my life. This has been my practice for a very long time. I do not have enough confidence in my knowledge of God's Word to believe that I would be incapable of being deceived. I never want to knowingly subject myself to anything that doesn't agree with scripture. Just as I would never eat a brownie or a bowl of soup that contained even 1% poison, I choose not to knowingly ingest anything into my mind that contains 1% poison.

It is my hope and prayer that this book will be a great blessing to some of you as we contemplate the events of this current day and age. My desire is to lift high God and His Word, while exposing the evil darkness that is cloaking itself as "wonderful" and "good" in the church today.

Learn to Discern

Preparing Your Heart and Mind

Before we can truly learn to discern, there are some things we need to give our attention to. Listed below are six ways that we should be growing in order to be an effective "discerner".

Here are six "**BEs**" that we should strive for–

1. BE Biblically Literate (In other words, *don't be ignorant of what the Bible teaches*)

My biggest regret–BY FAR–is not studying the Bible more in-depth earlier in my life. It is truly a treasure that is invaluable. The more you study it the more you realize this. We will not have the proper attitudes about discernment if we don't study the Bible. We will not know the truth to compare error to if we don't study the Bible. I would go so far as to say that without effort given to studying the Word of God, we really cannot be discerners at all.

2. BE Christ-Focused (In other words, *don't be "evil-world system" focused*)

It is so very easy to get caught up in all we are learning. As our eyes are opened and we start to see connections, for example, between well-known "pastors" and false religious systems or government agencies or we start to study some historical aspect of the church, the fascination of it all can be alluring. If we aren't careful, it can consume our thoughts and time. And so to be an effective discerner, we must keep our focus on Christ and His Word, first and foremost, *and* always.

3. BE Curious (In other words, *don't be apathetic*)

I see this one a lot. People who just don't care about spiritual things, which naturally leads to apathy about issues of discernment. But curiosity about what's going on and an interest in knowing (in order to protect, defend, and contend for the Word of God) is a must if we are to really learn to discern. Apathy is a thief of knowledge and the enemy of discernment.

4. BE Teachable (In other words, *don't think you have all of the answers*)

I would credit this one attitude to being one of the greatest assets in learning to discern. *When we think we know everything, we close our hearts to learning about anything.* This is true, whether we are talking about parenting, growing in biblical knowledge, or learning more about our career field. And it's also true regarding discernment. The sooner we recognize that we have an awful lot to learn, the sooner we will start learning.

5. BE Humble (in other words, *don't be proud*)

This is rather similar to being teachable, but goes even one step further in that this is an attitude that encompasses our whole being. If we are conceited, self-important, overbearing, argumentative, or pompous we not only limit our ability to learn, but we limit our ability to *share* what we have learned. When we aren't interested in the opinions or thoughts of others and always focusing on our own inflated opinions, we shut a door that is difficult to re-open.

6. **BE Observant** (In other words, *don't be naive*)

Yes, ignorance is sometimes bliss. But it is rarely a good thing in the long run. And so it is with discernment. How much better to know the truth so that we can protect ourselves and our loved ones from the wolves who look like sheep. It is imperative that we always keep our eyes open. I have to be honest here–the more I learn and realize the scope of the great deception in this age, the more skeptical I become. I don't take anything at face value but always do some research first. While we don't want to become hardened skeptics, it is important that we recognize the great invasion of false religion that is sweeping through the church. With this in mind, it is critical that we be Bereans, comparing all we see, read, watch, listen to–everything!–to the Holy Scriptures.

And so there are the six BEs–

> BE *biblically literate*
> BE *Bible-focused*
> BE *curious*
> BE *teachable*
> BE *humble*
> BE *observant*

If you have these things in place or are at least working at putting them in place, then you are ready to learn to discern!

What Is Biblical Christianity?

We really cannot learn to discern before we have a biblical definition of Christianity. There are so many warped, perverted, and bizarre religions out there taking on the name of Christ that it is almost unimaginable. But which is the true religion? As believers, we know that the Bible teaches that there is only one way for us to be reconciled to God (John 14:6). And we know that the Bible, from Genesis to Revelation, tells us the beautiful story of God's redemption of man and the salvation He offers to sinful man. We also find all we need to live in a way that pleases God in this troubled world (2 Timothy 3:16-17).

Please, please keep in mind as you read the essay below that these are the things true Christians desire. They will never be perfected on this side of heaven, but growth will take place and be evident in believers as we mature in Christ. A good question to ask ourselves is this: *Am I going in a direction towards God and His Word or away from God and His Word?*

I do want to be forthright about something. What is written below is in direct opposition to much of the popular religion called "Christianity" today. If we are going to be loyal to the Word of God, first and foremost, we must recognize this.

The following is written by my brother, Pastor Dean Good—

Who is a Christian? A quick Google search will tell us that the leading world religion is Christianity, numbering 2.1 billion people. Since the world population is 7.5 billion, almost one in three is classified as a Christian. But I am reminded of the words of Jesus who said *many will say to me in that day Lord, Lord . . . and then will I profess unto them, I never knew you: depart from Me, ye that work iniquity* (Matt. 7:22-23). The important point here is that self-classification is not the determining factor in answering the question *who is a Christian?* So perhaps we should ask who is a *true* Christian? Or rather, who does *Christ* classify as a Christian? That is the determining factor. Jesus said two things in the above quotation about false professors: (1) *I never knew you;* and (2) *you work iniquity.* No ungodly person unacquainted with the new birth will ever enter heaven. But let us consider positively what defines, according to Christ, a true Christian.

1. A True Christian Hears the Word of Christ. Jesus said: *Everyone that is of the truth hears My voice* (John 18:37); *My sheep hear My voice* (John 10:27); *He that is of God, hears God's words* (John 8:47). This is the most basic attribute of a true Christian. He receives, believes, trusts, obeys, and delights in God's Word, namely the Scriptures (Psalm 1:2; Psalm 119; Matt. 7:24-27; John 8:31-32; 17:8; 1 Thess. 2:13; 2 Thess. 2:13; James 1:21). This is called faith. The person who is apathetic, defiant, or careless toward Scripture is not a Christian according to Christ.

2. A True Christian Believes in Christ. Jesus said: *This is the work of God, that ye believe on Him whom He hath sent* (John 6:29); *He that believes on Me has everlasting life. I am the bread of life* (John 6:47-48). In view of the context of these verses, to believe on Christ is to believe at least two things about Christ. First, it is to believe that he is the Son of God, sent from the Father, and second, that He is the one who laid down His life, as the spotless Lamb of God, as an atonement for our sins. A Christian is one who has trusted in Christ alone for the forgiveness of his sins. He has been justified (declared righteous) by grace, through faith in the blood of Christ. He has been reconciled to God and, as a result, is at peace with God (Acts 13:38-39; Rom. 3:10-26; 5:1; Col. 1:20-23). Anyone who has not called upon the Lord for the forgiveness of his sins, through the blood of Christ, is not a Christian.

3. A True Christian Follows Christ. Jesus said: *My sheep hear My voice . . . and they follow Me* (John 10:27). In another place he said: *If any man will come after Me, let him deny himself, and take up his cross, and follow Me. For whosoever will save his life shall lose it: and whosoever will lose his life for My sake shall find it* (Matt. 16:24-25). Jesus said these words immediately after rebuking Peter for denying that he (i.e. Christ) must suffer and die. It is as if Jesus said, *Not only must I go to the cross, but so must you.* These words of Jesus are not a call to asceticism or martyrdom, but rather a call to regeneration. In order to live, you must die –to yourself, to sin, to your own desires. This saying of Jesus is closely related to Paul's words in Gal. 2:20: *I am crucified with Christ: nevertheless I live; yet not I, but Christ lives in me: and the life which I now live in the flesh I live by the faith of the Son of God, who loved me, and gave Himself for me.* You cannot be a Christian without dying to yourself. When we were born again, we died with Christ and arose with Christ (Rom. 6:2-4), therefore we are no longer slaves of sin but slaves of God (Rom. 6:22). We now live to please God in everything we do, say, and think. A Christian does not do this perfectly, but it is his desire. The person who is fundamentally living for himself, following his own dreams, pursuing his own pleasure is not a Christian, according to Christ.

4. A True Christian Has the Spirit Of Christ. Jesus said: *I will pray the Father, and He shall give you another*

Comforter, that He may abide with you forever; even the Spirit of truth; whom the world cannot receive, because it seeth Him not, neither knoweth Him; but ye know Him; for He dwelleth with you and shall be in you (Jn. 14:16-17). Paul wrote: *Now if any man have not the Spirit of Christ, he is none of His* (Rom. 8:9). A true Christian is a temple of the Holy Spirit and where the Holy Spirit dwells there will be evidences. The Spirit produces holiness in the life. By holiness I do not mean merely morality. Many unbelievers are at some level moral. Holiness is an inward delight in God, His Word, His will, His plan, and His people. This holiness can further be described as the fruit of the Spirit: *love, joy, peace, long-suffering, gentleness, goodness, faith, meekness, and temperance* (Gal. 5:22-23). Of course, a true Christian is by no means perfect in regard to these qualities and in fact he daily struggles with sin in his own heart. But where this holy character is fundamentally lacking, we can be certain the Holy Spirit is not present. Such a person, according to Christ, is not a Christian.

5. A True Christian Loves the Body of Christ. Jesus said: *By this shall all men know that you are My disciples, if you have love one to another* (Jn. 13:35). Jesus was not merely speaking of a general love for people. He was referring to love within the body of Christ. A defining mark of a Christian is love for fellow-believers. John wrote: *We know that we have passed from death unto life because we love the brethren* (1 Jn. 3:14). A true Christian serves the church of Jesus Christ. He bears the burdens of fellow-believers. He attends upon the preaching of the Word and the Christ-ordained ordinances in the context of the local church. A person who does not delight in God's people and forsakes the gathering of the saints, is not a Christian by Biblical standards.

6. A True Christian Perseveres in Christ. Jesus said: *If you continue in My word, then are you My disciples indeed* (John 8:31). There are many who seem to follow Christ for a time. This was true in Christ's day (John 2:23-25; 6:66), it was true in the Apostle John's experience (1 John 2:19), and it is true today. There are many who ostensibly receive the Word with much joy, but then wither at the first sign of persecution, or become, over time, utterly choked out by the cares of this world and the deceitfulness of riches (Matt. 13:18-22). Such are not true Christians. They may take the name, but they are not classified as Christians by Christ. A true Christian perseveres through trials, difficulties, failures, temptations, and struggles. He may fall down a thousand times, but by the grace of God, he keeps following Christ.

Jesus said that in order to enter the kingdom of heaven we must enter by the narrow gate and walk by the narrow way (Matt. 7:13-14). We are told that we must through much tribulation enter the kingdom of God (Acts 14:22). Jesus said that many will seek to enter the kingdom but will not be able (Luke 13:24).

These are sobering words. Yet his promises are as sure as they have ever been. He has given us everything we need in his Word for life and godliness (2 Pet. 1:3-4). Let us be prayerful, humble, diligent, trembling, faithful, believing, obedient, life-long students of the Word of God, for this is the means by which God keeps his children (Proverbs 2:1-22). This is how we look to Christ.

Finally, a Christian is one who loves Christ. We love Him because we know that whatever good is in us is the result of His work. If left to myself, I would be lost. But Jesus saved me. This is a true Christian.

Learn to Discern

The Corruption of Christianity

What in the world is going on in the church today? It is a question many believers are asking. And, in fact, it has changed so much in the past fifty years or so that it has become almost unrecognizable when compared to the church of old. Of course, we need to remember that *old* is not necessarily *better* and so it is critical that we compare all that is going on around us, both in the world and in the church, to what scripture teaches.

In this chapter, Pastor Dean will give us a great biblical overview of six transitions that are leading the church into apostasy at an alarming rate. These things have corrupted Christianity until it is almost beyond recognition when compared to the Word of God. While all of these have probably been around in one form or another since Christianity began, there is now a fierce, all-out onslaught of all six going on. In fact, you are going to recognize many of these. They are found in your churches; in Christian books, music, and movies;

and in many of the Bible Studies you have done. You will hear fellow believers discuss these things as if they are biblical and you will hear of them on the mission field. Many sincere pastors, authors, and others have been deceived into believing these things are true and good. However, when we look at what scripture teaches, we can see that they aren't from God at all. Instead, they are man's wisdom, often cloaked in biblical terminology, and originating from Satan himself.

And let's not forget one very important thing: *A one-world religion is coming*. Everything that is going on is leading the "church" to join this religion. It is like we can see this taking place right before our very eyes.

I believe what is found below, written by Pastor Dean Good, will be extremely helpful to all of us as we seek to honor God and be discerning believers--

The Bible warns a great deal of false prophets, false teachers, false Christs, false brethren, false teaching and false gospels. In fact, we are told that there will be, at the end of the age, a false church that is an apostate church. One that has a form of godliness, one that has all the trappings of Christianity, one that speaks of Christ, calls Him Lord, uses all the Biblical lingo, claims powerful spiritual experiences, and yet is *utterly deceived and lost*. This apostate church will help to unify the world around the Antichrist (2 Thess. 2:3-12). It will be defined as a church that has fundamentally rejected the truth.

The evangelical church of today is very quickly descending into an apostate condition. This descent runs across all denominational and theological lines. In some ways it is difficult to quantify this plunge because it involves so many facets. There is a complexity to its development, because its roots are traced to New Testament times (2 Thess. 2:7) and, before that, to ancient Babylon, and all the way back to the Garden of Eden. But various movements of the 20th and early 21st centuries have converged into a perfect storm hurling the professing church into an utterly worldly, confused, degenerate state. There are at least six transitions that have taken place in this gradual, yet rapid corruption of the church. In this brief chapter they can only be introduced.

1. THE CORRUPTION OF WORSHIP: From Preaching to Entertainment. True worship according to Scripture is hearing God's Word. What does it mean to hear God's Word? It means to believe it, receive it in meekness, meditate on it, tremble at it, obey it, trust it, submit to it, delight in it, and proclaim it (cf. Prov. 28:9; Is. 66:1-3). Since this is true, the highest form of public worship is the preaching of the Word (2 Tim. 4:1-2). But serious, reverent, God-fearing preachers have been replaced by motivational speakers, rock bands, comedians, puppets, dancers, and drama teams. This transition from the simple and consistent preaching of the Word to a highly choreographed production took place over many decades, but has now reached the point of absurdity. But Paul warned us of such a day (2 Tim. 4:3-4).

2. THE CORRUPTION OF THE MESSAGE: From the Cross to Self-Actualization. The central message of the church is the cross. There are two aspects to this message: (1) Christ died on the cross to make an atonement for our sins to deliver us from death and Hell (1 Pet. 1:18-19); and (2) when we believe on Christ we are united with Him in His death and resurrection (Rom. 6:3-4) and are called to follow Christ in the way of the cross (Matt. 16:24-26). As Christians who have been born again, we are dead to sin and alive to God and are called to die daily to our lusts through the renewing of our minds. This is summarized in Paul's statement in Gal. 2:20 – *I am crucified with Christ: nevertheless I live; yet not I, but Christ lives in me: and the life which I now live in the flesh I live by the faith of the Son of God, who loved me, and gave Himself for me.* This central message has been subtly replaced by the psychologized message of self-actualization. Christ has become our divine psychologist who wants to heal our hurts and pain, fix our broken and dysfunctional relationships, and give us a positive feeling about ourselves so that we can live fulfilled lives. This psychobabble was largely borrowed from psychologists Carl Rogers and Abraham Maslow, as well as "Pastor" Norman Vincent Peale and has resulted in a self-centered, self-loving, self-pitying, non-serving generation of churchgoers who see themselves as victims of psychological disorders and diseases rather than offenders of God's Law, fundamentally needing healing and purpose rather than mercy and forgiveness.

3. THE CORRUPTION OF SPIRITUALITY: From Faith to Mysticism. Biblical faith is simply belief in the Word of God that results in trust and obedience. Abraham is the great example of faith. God gave him a promise and a command (Gen. 12:1-3) and because he believed God's promise, he obeyed God's command (Heb. 11:8). The whole Christian life operates on the principle of Biblical faith (Col. 2:5-7), which is dependent on a rational understanding and growing knowledge of Scripture (Rom. 12:1-2; 2 Pet. 3:18). But the new paradigm has replaced faith with mysticism. Mysticism is direct communion with God apart from the rational. The Christian life is now founded on, defined by, measured by, and consumed with subjective, sensual, tangible, palpable, sentimental emotions, feelings, and experiences. Personal visions, revelations, signs from heaven, impressions from the Spirit, messages from God, and heart-warming encounters are the new standard. These are the measure of truth, the means of spiritual growth, and the source of assurance of God's presence. All of these experiences are, of course, justified with an attached Bible verse. Serious, analytical Bible study and sound theology are deemed cold rationalism, dead orthodoxy, and the quenching of the Spirit, all the Scriptural warnings notwithstanding. This transition has opened the doors of the church to almost any false teaching in vogue at any given time. Like a body without an immune system, the church has been overrun by every theological virus known to mankind. Yet the patient has no sense of his condition.

4. THE CORRUPTION OF LEADERSHIP: From Shepherd to CEO. The leaders of the church, according to Scripture, are shepherds (1 Peter 5:1-4). They are to humbly feed and lead the flock of God by the patient and prayerful preaching, teaching, and administering of the Word of God. Leading by example, they are to be men of godly character who demonstrate a father-like concern and mother-like gentleness in caring for the local church (1 Thess. 2:1-12). This Biblical model of leadership has been replaced by the worldly model of the corporate CEO. With the advent of the Church Growth Movement and the Purpose Driven Movement, pastors have taken on a thoroughly pragmatic view of leadership. Creating top-down organizational structures, and wielding management, psychological, and marketing techniques, they have manipulated the sheep to accomplish their self-promoting agendas. The prophet Ezekiel gave us a poignant portrait of these modern shepherds (Ez. 34:1-10). This corruption of church leadership has resulted in a massive increase in numbers and a correspondingly comprehensive death of Biblical spirituality. Indeed, the sheep have been scattered and devoured because they have no shepherds (Ez. 34:5-6).

5. THE CORRUPTION OF MISSION: From the Gospel to the Social Gospel. The church has only one mission to the world: To preach the Gospel (Matt. 28:19-20). We are calling the world to repent of their sins and believe on the Lord Jesus Christ. We are calling them to flee the wrath to come and find refuge in the Savior. You will search the Scriptures in vain to find any call to social action or social reform. But the evangelical church today is consumed with transforming the world, fighting poverty, bringing racial harmony, working toward world peace, saving the environment, and all other forms of social justice. Instead of seeking the salvation from sin of individual souls through faith in the gospel, the church is seeking the salvation of the society from social ills through community action and government intervention. This is a revival of the Liberal Theology of the late 19th and early 20th centuries and has resulted in the death of the gospel. Many who are promoting social justice give lip service to the gospel, but where the social gospel takes hold, the gospel of Jesus Christ will always eventually be choked out. They are incompatible.

6. THE CORRUPTION OF FELLOWSHIP: From Separation to Ecumenism. The Bible calls us to love the brethren and preserve the unity of the Spirit, but to separate ourselves from the world (2 Cor. 6:14-18) and from apostates (2 Thess. 3:14). True Biblical unity is the work of the Holy Spirit and cannot be accomplished by politics, networking, and ecumenical declarations. The dual unity (with believers) and separation (from unbelievers) commanded in Scripture is accomplished through clear, consistent, thorough teaching of Biblical truth (Eph. 4:11-16). This does not mean that we are to be unkind or ungracious toward unbelievers or that we can have no interaction with the world (1 Cor. 6:9-10), but rather that we must acknowledge we have no spiritual union or fellowship with them and should separate ourselves from all ungodly and foolish lusts (1 Pet. 4:2-4) and all manner of heresies (Titus 3:10). But the church has increasingly embraced every manner of worldliness and foolishness in the name of evangelism, and has welcomed heretics, false teachers, shysters, and rogues of every kind, in the name of Biblical unity. The evangelical church is linking arms with Liberals, Roman Catholics, Mormons, Eastern Orthodox, and even Muslims and Atheists in the name of unity and social change, even though all these groups reject justification by grace alone through faith alone in Christ alone and according to the Apostle Paul are accursed (Gal. 1:6-9). We do not say this out of hate, but out of love, knowing that no man will ever enter heaven apart from faith and repentance, and the acknowledging of the truth in Jesus Christ.

There is a sense in which the first five transitions, in their cumulative effect, have brought about the sixth transition of ecumenical unity. The Ecumenical Movement is like a funnel almost irresistibly drawing everyone toward the euphoric and blind Satanic unity of the last days apostate church. Let us put on the full armor of God (Eph. 6:10-18) through the diligent study of, and obedience to, the Word of God. Let us separate from all that is false and ungodly. Let us keep ourselves in the love of God (Jude 20-21) always remembering that it is God who keeps us from falling and will present us faultless before the presence of His glory with exceeding joy (Jude 24).

What Is Your Paradigm?

Paradigm is defined as a framework from which a person judges all of life around them. This seems like an appropriate base to lay before we biblically examine the specific worldviews, philosophies, and theologies that are being promoted within and without the church.

Every single one of us has a paradigm. We all have a belief system through which we judge all of life. We judge speakers, authors, and entertainers. We judge events, churches, and workplaces. We judge family, friends, and co-workers all through this framework. We may not like the word "judge" but we all do judge.

Think with me for a moment about the far left who are touting tolerance and love. Do they judge? They most certainly do! From their paradigm, they view Bible believers as unintellectual, ridiculous, and even "nut jobs". This is a *judgment*.

As believers, we should naturally have a very different paradigm than those who are not believers. Man's wisdom and God's wisdom are in opposition to one another.

I Corinthians 2:13-16 makes this very clear–

These things we also speak, not in words which man's wisdom teaches but which the Holy[d] Spirit teaches, comparing spiritual things with spiritual. 14 But the natural man does not receive the things of the Spirit of God, for they are foolishness to him; nor can he know them, because they are spiritually discerned. 15 But he who is spiritual judges all things, yet he himself is rightly judged by no one. 16 For "who has known the mind of the Lord that he may instruct Him?"[e] But we have the mind of Christ.

As does I Corinthians 3:18-20—

Let no one deceive himself. If anyone among you seems to be wise in this age, let him become a fool that he may become wise. 19 For the wisdom of this world is foolishness with God. For it is written, "He catches the wise in their own craftiness"; [a] 20 and again, "The Lord knows the thoughts of the wise, that they are futile.

Along with this passage in James 3:13-17—

Who is wise and understanding among you? Let him show by good conduct that his works are done in the meekness of wisdom. [14] But if you have bitter envy and self-seeking in your hearts, do not boast and lie against the truth. [15] This wisdom does not descend from above, but is earthly, sensual, demonic. [16] For where envy and self-seeking exist, confusion and every evil thing are there. [17] But the wisdom that is from above is first pure, then peaceable, gentle, willing to yield, full of mercy and good fruits, without partiality and without hypocrisy.

Worldly wisdom and biblical wisdom, being in such contrast to one another, should never and, in fact, *can never* be joined to one another. They are intrinsically incompatible.

This makes for a very difficult problem for those who would call themselves Christian but desire to follow after the world's wisdom, would it not?

(An important thing to insert here: I am not referring to the God-given knowledge that leads to inventions, medical breakthroughs, and the like. When I refer to "man's wisdom", I am referring to man's philosophies and values; his answers to life's biggest questions.)

If you think back to what you read in the last chapter, you will remember that there are six ways the world has infiltrated the church. Each one of these is based on the world's wisdom rather than God's wisdom. This is because men declare themselves to be wiser than the Word of God.

But if we are genuine, thoughtful believers, it is critical that we recognize that our only source for absolute truth is in God's Word, the Holy Scriptures.

This leads us to understand that there are, in fact, only two ways to interpret the world–

There is the *biblical paradigm*, where one's framework for life is drawn from the pages of scripture and everything is viewed and processed through this grid of God's Word.

And there is the *worldly paradigm*, where one's framework for life is based on human wisdom, and where the wisdom of men and women who are designated scientists, philosophers, and spiritual leaders are considered to be of more value than the Word of God.

And let's be clear: ***Our paradigm changes everything***.

One of the most obvious places this is taking place is in the battle for the beginning. On one hand, you have a scientist who starts with the Bible's historical account of creation. From this viewpoint, the past is then interpreted. He will provide solid and clear answers based on the Word of God for some of the past's toughest questions and quandaries. On the other hand, you have a scientist who holds man's word to be of higher value than God's Word. He then bases his assumptions of the earth's beginnings on the theories of men. From these assumptions are born calculations and models and principles that end up being passed on as *facts* (they aren't facts, they are assumptions) by teachers, science journals, and museums. Can you see how each one's paradigm leads to two completely different and opposing viewpoints of the world's beginning? This is just one example of how our paradigm leads to completely different conclusions about the world around us.

Now why is this important regarding discernment?

Because if you do not have the proper paradigm, you will not be able to discern biblically. As believers, we know that the Word of God is living and powerful (Hebrews 4:12) and that the faith has been delivered to us once for all (Jude 3). We also know that it is *by the scriptures* that we learn about Christ (Romans 16:26) and that God's Word is perfect (Psalm 19:7) and God-breathed (2 Timothy 3:16).

There is so much more that could be said about the Word of God. For it is only through the Word that we can know God, that we can understand salvation, and that we can learn proper doctrine. Not only is this our only resource, it is utterly sufficient to do all of this. We do not need any other resource or experience outside of the Word in order to know God.

But a new paradigm has crept into the church. It actually isn't all that new but is, instead, the same old humanistic paradigm of old. In this framework, the authority and inerrancy of scripture is being removed and oh-so-subtly being replaced with man's wisdom. Subjective experiences and feelings are becoming the standard for truth, while biblical doctrine is downplayed or even eliminated altogether. This paradigm relies on interpreting the scriptures allegorically, out-of-context, and/or non-literally–if it even uses scripture at all. It holds man's word to be of higher value than God's Word. And it leads to a man-centered religion rather than a God-centered religion.

It is critical for us to have a biblical paradigm if we desire to discern effectively. Do you believe that the Bible is the authoritative, inerrant, and inspired Word of God? Do you believe that all of life must be evaluated through the grid of the Bible? If you have answered *yes* to these two questions, then you are ready to "learn to discern".

Philosophies in Opposition

There are some very obvious differences between mainstream "Christianity" (which is informed by humanistic philosophies and worldly thinking) and biblical Christianity (which is based on the inerrant and inspired Holy Bible). When we take some time to carefully evaluate this, we see that they aren't merely different but are, in fact, in *complete opposition* to one another. This has happened so subtly and so gradually that many of us haven't picked up on it.

For example, many years ago I read a novel. When I was through with it, I read the whole series. I loved every single book in that series. Since then, I have grown stronger in learning to discern. When I picked up this same book a year or two ago, I saw it for what it was: An engaging story that encouraged nice Christian ladies right on into *mysticism*.

But I didn't see it the first time. I didn't see it because I didn't know the Word of God like I should have and, also, because I had no idea how subtle and crafty Satan was (and *is*) in his all-out attack on all things Christian.

In this chapter will take a look at some of the common philosophies that Mainstream "Christianity" is endorsing and compare these to what the Bible teaches. This exercise will be of great value as we learn to discern.

Here is a short list of some of the lies advanced by Mainstream "Christianity". This is not an exhaustive list and please keep in mind that not all who are caught up in this false religion are teaching all of these. It will vary from author to author and church to church. But here are TEN WAYS that Biblical Christianity finds itself in opposition to Mainstream (or Pop) Christianity—

1. Mainstream says <u>Find Your Purpose and Fulfill Your Dreams.</u>

The Bible says to surrender everything to Jesus and live only for Him. *Matthew 10:28-29; Matthew 16:25; John 12:24-25; Philippians 3:7-10*

2. Mainstream says that <u>Unity is the Ultimate Goal.</u>

The Bible says that unity without truth is not true unity. *Matthew 10:34-35; Romans 16:17-18; I John 4:1-3; Galatians 1:8*

3. Mainstream says that <u>The Church's Purpose is to Help the Poor.</u>

The Bible tells us the church's purpose is to teach the Word and share the Gospel. *Matthew 28:18-20; Acts 2:42; Titus 1:7-10*

4. Mainstream says that <u>We Need to Make the World a Better Place.</u>

The Bible makes it clear that this world will never be a better place. *Matthew 24; 2 Thessalonians 2:1-12; 2 Timothy 3:1-9*

5. Mainstream says that <u>We Need to Experience God in Order to Be Close to Him.</u>

The Bible tells us that we grow closer to God by submitting to Him and obeying His Word. *John 14:15; John 15:10; Romans 6:16; James 4:7 ; I Peter 5:6; I John 2:3-6*

6. Mainstream says that <u>We Should Expect Special Revelation from God.</u>

The Bible teaches that it alone is sufficient for all we need. *Psalm 19:7-14; 2 Timothy 3:15-17; Jude 1:3*

7. Mainstream says we must <u>Be Like the World to Win the World.</u>

The Bible tells us we are to separate ourselves from the world. *John 15:18-21; Romans 12:2; James 4:4; I John 2:15-17*

8. Mainstream says <u>We Must Learn to Love Ourselves.</u>

The Bible tells us, as we already do love ourselves, we must learn to love others. *Matthew 22:39; Mark 12:31; Ephesians 5:29*

9. Mainstream says that <u>Christ's Sacrifice Covers Everyone in the Whole World, No Matter Their Religion (the term for this is *Universalism*).</u>

The Bible tells us that we must personally call on Jesus to be saved. *John 3:16; John 3:36; John 14:6; Romans 10:9*

10. Mainstream says <u>YOU Are the Center of Your Religion.</u>

The Bible teaches that it is God who is the center of true religion; it is God alone who gets the glory. *Romans 11:36; I Corinthians 10:31; Philippians 2:9-11*

So you have just read through a list of ten major philosophies that are in clear opposition to one another. Of course, most pastors, authors, and song-writers are not coming right out and saying these things. Instead, they are carefully and cunningly using out-of-context Bible verses to craft these spiritual-sounding philosophies. They are preying on a people who do not know their Bibles and are even less informed about church history. The lack of understanding of these two things has left the church defenseless. Utterly defenseless.

And if we don't know our Bibles, we can most certainly understand how easily it would be to be swayed. What they teach sounds *really good.* Who wouldn't want a religion that is all about them? That feeds their own lusts and desires and dreams, while still giving lip service to a Holy God and a fire insurance policy from eternal damnation?

The overall appeal of these philosophies, combined with the fact that there has been a major push to make these a part of the mainstream, evangelical church, is making them hard to resist. These beliefs have totally changed the church from the inside out. So much so that now, when we declare them to be anti-God and in opposition to God's Word, we are viewed as divisive and narrow-minded and irrelevant.

But please do not be deceived. Truth and popularity are generally mutually exclusive. I know that it is so much easier to follow the crowd. But in today's

Christian culture, following the crowd will lead us right off the cliff. The church is moving closer and closer to being swallowed up by the coming one-world religion and the subtle, appealing, and *extreme* differences in philosophies are paving the way.

The level of deception is so great now that it's hard to believe. In some form or another, many of these philosophies--under the leadership of unsuspecting pastors who truly want to do what's right--have entered the doors of even the most conservative of churches. And they have entered many homes under the watchful, albeit naïve, eyes of parents who think they are helping and guiding their kids.

And, while we can't control the direction of evangelicalism, we *can* protect ourselves and our families from these lies. We can understand some of these basic philosophical differences. As we become familiar with these major differences and learn what to look for, we will find these things start to show themselves everywhere we turn. No, we can't change the direction of the crowd headed for the cliff, but we *can* work to keep these philosophies from entering our own hearts and minds, our families, and our churches.

Not only does the spiritual health of a believer hang in the balance with these false teachings running rampant, but the very salvation of those who would believe may also hang in the balance. While we recognize that it is God who draws and saves, it is also of value to consider how false teaching blinds the eyes and deafens the ears of so many.

It is my hope and prayer that this little book will awaken someone to the dangers and deception going on in the modern day church and that it will embolden them to teach those in their own circle, as well as impassion their zeal to witness to those who need Jesus so desperately.

Acknowledging the War

Have you ever heard someone deny that the holocaust occurred? It seems almost preposterous, but I have heard that theory go around more than once. But denying that it happened doesn't change the truth, does it?

So far, we have learned what true, biblical Christianity is; we have learned how biblical Christianity is being corrupted; we have learned the importance of using scripture to give us a biblical paradigm; and we have learned that we must never follow man over the Word of God.

In this chapter, we are going to focus on the importance of acknowledging that there is a spiritual war going on. Just like the holocaust existed whether someone chooses to believe it or chooses not to believe it, so, too, does a spiritual war. Denying or ignoring it doesn't change the fact that *there is one.*

Years ago, we Christians would sing songs like **Onward, Christian Soldiers**—

> *Onward, Christian soldiers,*
> *marching as to war,*
> *With the cross of Jesus*
> *going on before!*
> *Christ, the royal Master,*
> *leads against the foe;*
> *Forward into battle,*
> *see his banner go!*

and **Stand Up, Stand Up for Jesus**—

> *Stand up, stand up for Jesus,*
> *Ye soldiers of the cross;*
> *Lift high his royal banner,*
> *It must not suffer loss.*
> *From victory unto victory*
> *His army shall he lead,*
> *Till every foe is vanquished,*
> *And Christ is Lord indeed.*

But as the church started to change, we stopped singing songs like these. There was no longer a desire to focus on anything negative or unhappy. Instead of being focused on *all* truth found in scripture, it became a religion that was focused on positivity and happiness. All negativity was pushed to the side, while the church changed its focus to bringing happiness and goodness to the world.

Of course, there is nothing wrong with doing good things, particularly if we are also sharing the unadulterated Gospel or encouraging a fellow believer. But when we become focused *only* on this, we are ignoring much of the Bible.

Hell (*Mark 9:43; Matthew 25:41*); prophecy (*Daniel, Matthew 24, Revelation*); self-denial and personal sacrifice (*Matthew 16:24, Luke 9:23, Romans 12:1*); separating from the world (*Romans 12:2, James 1:27*); and other doctrines and commands that are viewed as "negative" have been and continue to be, by and large, ignored.

And so, too, has the reality that there is a spiritual war that we are fighting every day of our lives. We are fighting battles--

- Against the world (*2 Corinthians 10:3-5*).

- Against ourselves (*Galatians 5:17*).

- Against Satan and his demons (*Ephesians 6:10-20*).

What does this have to do with discernment, you may ask? The answer to this is simple: *If we don't recognize that there is a war going on, we will not see the need to discern.*

By the way, it is easy to ignore this spiritual war. Oh, so very easy.

First, as I have already mentioned, most of us never hear anything about it. It is, by and large, ignored by our churches and by those who would profess Christ, as a whole. We also have to admit that, for most of us, if it's out of sight, it is also out of mind.

Second, we are too busy and distracted to be concerned. We fill our schedules with the mundane and declare ourselves too busy to be in the Word, which is the only place to get a full understanding of the war we are in. Yes, some of you are most definitely overwhelmed in an incredibly busy time of life. I've been there! But all of us have little pockets of time we find for what is important. Is reading and studying the Bible on your short list of priorities?

And, **third**, we just don't want to think about it. Life is full of enough unpleasantries–things like stress at work, broken relationships, our own sinful habits–who needs to think about an over-arching spiritual war on top of all of these things? We want to be entertained. We want to think on happy things. We want to be comforted and coddled. We certainly don't want to spend time thinking about a war we are fighting.

But whether we think about it or not, it is there. In the spiritual realm. It is there *every single minute of every single day*.

Being aware of this war changes how we view almost everything, quite honestly. For example—

• If we recognize that the latest and greatest "Christian" book may be a tool used by Satan to harden our conscience or to change how we view God, we will do our research before just picking it up to read it.

• If we know that the latest children's movie may well be full of ungodly philosophies, we will keep our eyes open and discuss these things with our kids, using the scriptures or, better yet, we may choose not to allow them to watch it at all.

• If we understand that Satan hates the true Church and realize that he is doing everything in his power to infiltrate it as he seeks to bring about a one-world religion, then we will be much more apt to notice the red flags of human wisdom and mysticism that enter our church doors.

When we understand there is a deadly, spiritual war going on, *all things* will be carefully examined before we allow ourselves or those we love to just blindly ingest or indulge in them.

Many people just don't want to learn to discern. They view it with disdain, believing it to be an unnecessary evil. But if we recognize the war, how can we help but desire to discern?

We don't discern because we are unpleasant and unhappy people. It isn't that we hate entertainment, in and of itself. It certainly isn't that we desire to be negative. And it's not that we hate the Church and its dear people.

We discern because we love Christ's Church. We discern because we understand the spiritual danger that comes when we choose not to discern. Danger that is both to ourselves and our fellow believers, whom we dearly love. And we discern because we understand there is a war going on--a deadly war that is taking many casualties. This war is keeping many from hearing the true Gospel and it is de-sensitizing true believers, rendering them completely ineffective for the cause of Christ.

We must fight this war with the only weapon we have and the only one we need, which is the holy and perfect Word of God (Ephesians 6:17).

Dear readers, please be aware of this war. For it is only through this awareness, that we can be effective and godly discerners.

How Do You Determine What Is True, Right, and Good?

How often have you heard something like the following as a defense for a false teacher or a doctrinally unsound book or church?

"But it has helped so many people!"

Or even more personally--

"It has really helped (or is really helping) me."

The item or person in question is judged on this fact alone: If it has helped someone, it must be right. And if it hasn't helped anyone, then it must be wrong.

But here is something we must consider: Is this how the Bible teaches us to determine truth? Does the fact that something is helpful automatically make it true, right, or good?

The belief that this is how we determine truth is called **pragmatism.**

Officially, the definition for **pragmatism** is: *An approach that assesses the truth of meaning of theories or beliefs in terms of the success of their practical application.*

In essence, it is the belief that the end justifies the means.

Most of us would say, of course, this isn't true. We would never agree that we can get from point A to point B any way we want to. But, when it comes to how we actually approach what is true, we have taken on this philosophy far more than we would care to admit.

For example, when the book *The Shack* first came out, many, many Christians loved it. If anyone dared to suggest it wasn't doctrinally sound, the defense was that "it helped me understand who God is" or "it comforted me."

Of course, we can see that the measurement being used by most people to judge this book was a practical, subjective method (how it makes me feel or what I have perceived) rather than using scripture as the measurement tool.

Many years later, William Paul Young clearly demonstrated that He does not believe what the Bible teaches in his book, *Lies We Believe About God.* In this book, he clearly denies tenet after tenet of the Christian faith.

So why were so many Christians fooled? Why did they not recognize this early on? And why did it take a book that finally clearly espouses what he believes to convince them?

For many, it is because they are pragmatists. They judge what is right and what is wrong by what works for them or by what feels right or good.

I guess it is only natural that this would eventually enter even the most conservative churches. After all, it started in the secular culture a while ago now.

It is so important that if we are going to learn to discern, we do not fall prey to this deadly philosophy.

In order to protect ourselves it is critical that we learn what scripture teaches us about how we determine truth. Let's take a look–

John 17:17 *Sanctify them in the truth; Thy word is truth.*

In this chapter, Jesus is praying for believers. He is asking the Father to protect and keep us. And to sanctify us. And He adds this interesting line: *Thy word is truth.* The Bible is truth.

In 2 Timothy we find another verse showing us that the Word is truth–

2 Timothy 2:15 *Do your best to present yourself to God as one approved, a worker who has no need to be ashamed, rightly handling the word of truth.*

From these two verses, we can see that <u>the Bible is truth.</u>

Now let's take a moment and look at a few verses that clearly show we will not be the popular ones, the successful ones, and that it will appear our methods are *not* working (at least according to human, worldly standards)–

Romans 12:2 *Do not be conformed to this world, but be transformed by the renewal of your mind, that by testing you may discern what is the will of God, what is good and acceptable and perfect.*

Luke 6:26 *Woe to you, when all people speak well of you, for so their fathers did to the false prophets.*

James 4:4 *You adulterous people! Do you not know that friendship with the world is enmity with God? Therefore, whoever wishes to be a friend of the world makes himself an enemy of God.*

Matthew 7:13-14 *Enter by the narrow gate; for wide is the gate and broad is the way that leads to destruction, and there are many who go in by it. Because narrow is the gate and difficult is the way which leads to life, and there are few who find it.*

We can know from the above verses that true believers will generally not be favored and followed. (Generally. There are exceptions, of course.) Therefore, even when we are faithfully following God and doing as He commands us in His Word, it will often appear as if what we are doing is "not working". And, because we are basically told both inside and outside the church that "if it isn't working, God isn't in it", we are tempted to measure ourselves by the success we experience in the mainstream church or the world, rather than by using the barometer of scripture.

I would also like to remind you that Satan has to make false teachers look appealing. If he didn't, no one would follow them. Therefore, the indication that their methods or ministries seem to be working according to human standards should never be our measurement of what is true, right, or good.

Of course, there are also the real-life experiences of Jesus, Paul, Jeremiah, and of countless others throughout the history of the world to also assure us that what we are doing will not always appear to be working. Followers deserted Jesus (John 6:66), Paul was attacked by the crowds (Acts 16:22-24), and Jeremiah's pleas for change did not work (Jeremiah 44:4-5). Research a little church history or read a few missionary biographies and you will find many more examples of this.

From this we can conclude that we should never judge whether or not something is true, right, or good by the method of pragmatism. Instead, we must always turn to scripture as our litmus test for what is true, right, and good. The Bible is the only thing we need as we *learn to discern*.

Who Do You Follow?

In chapter six, we talked about understanding our paradigm. When we have established our paradigm, it would seem that we would naturally know who to follow. But what I have discovered is that the loyalty to fallible men (and women) runs so deeply that eventually many find themselves saying with their mouths that they adhere to the Word of God as the ultimate source of truth while their actions actually negate their assertions.

Here are a few examples–

Take the books *Jesus Calling* and *The Shack*. I choose these two, in particular, because they have been two of the most dangerous and influential "Christian" books, each of them undermining long-held biblical doctrines and replacing them with unbiblical, mystical beliefs. These books are promoted by Christians, they are sold in Christian bookstores, and they are touted as wonderful Christian books. But when both of these books are carefully examined, we can see that they go completely against critical biblical doctrines. Not sort of. Not kind of. But *completely*.

And yet, thousands–maybe millions–of Christians who claim to love and honor the Word of God speak highly of these books! Why is this? It is because they have chosen to value a human author's word more highly than God's Word.

Another example would be the response of some people when someone speaks up regarding the compromise of a beloved author or teacher. Instead of thoughtfully considering and comparing what is being taught by this person to what the Bible teaches, they immediately grow angry and defensive of this person that they have come to count on for solid, biblical teaching. And, once again, we see that they have placed a man's word before the Word of God.

A final example is found in churches across the world. Preachers start to twist and change important doctrines, but they are so beloved by most church members that there is a conscious choice to overlook the compromise rather than to remove themselves from false teaching. Loyalty to a man becomes more important than loyalty to God.

People are naturally loyal. They naturally want to trust teachers, authors, musicians, and preachers. We even find this same dynamic in the landscape business that my husband and I own. Most customers are loyal. They choose to trust us. And this is a good thing for business. And, quite honestly, this type of loyalty can sometimes be good in the church, too. It is never wise to leave a church or to choose to stop listening to a preacher or reading the books of an author because of some minor difference of opinion that is unrelated to scriptural truth. And even minor differences on secondary biblical doctrines are bound to occur and can be overlooked. The issue here is when major biblical doctrines are compromised. And I am so disheartened that this appears to be happening with popular "Christian" authors and teachers at such an exponential rate that it is almost impossible to comprehend.

I honestly believe that this dynamic of human loyalty is one of Satan's sharpest tools in his toolbox of devices used to bring false doctrine into the church. Take, for example, something that happened at a church I attended years ago. The youth group started showing videos by Rob Bell. Even in those early years, Bell was saying some very troublesome, unbiblical things. And, yet, if anyone dared to say anything against these videos, they were immediately labeled. They were *hyper-critical*. They were *negative*. They were *nit-picking* (you know—all those labels that are used when one dares to speak up). There was some type of loyalty to Rob Bell and his engaging, very well-done videos and speaking up against them only yielded criticism and antagonism.

And yet, only a few short years later, Rob Bell showed his true colors by denying several essential biblical doctrines. At this point, many quickly stopped following him. But the damage had already been done. Impressionable youth listened to him espouse on spiritual things and probably went on to follow him.

Following the wrong person is downright dangerous. It not only puts our own spiritual health at risk, but those who trust our judgment are also put at risk.

A few years ago, I placed a link on the *Growing4Life* website to a ministry that I believed to be a sound in its teaching. I found out a year or two later that, while they were teaching many good things, the ministry itself was steeped in mysticism. I removed the link immediately. This ministry was not trustworthy and, although I had grown to love this ministry, I quickly removed it from my website and chose to discontinue following them. Oh, how I hope that I was not responsible for leading any of my readers to that ministry and into mysticism!

Loyalty without biblical examination is never wise. And in both of the examples above–the Bell videos and the link on my blog–this did not happen. Loyalty came *before* proper examination and may very well have led someone down the wrong path.

I know there are some of you who are inevitably going to ask: *Why not just pick through the good stuff of a teacher or author and discard the heresies?* I will tell you three important reasons why I choose not to do this and would encourage you to do the same–

1. I do not believe that I am so spiritually mature that I could discern all of the error if I listened to someone who isn't teaching truth. I just don't know the Bible *that* well. If they are blatantly teaching against scripture in one area, what will keep them from doing so in another? And if they are, do I know the Bible well enough to actually spot it?

2. There are so many good things out there, why waste my time on picking through half-truths? If you have the choice between a fresh corn on the cob where every kernel is sweet and delicious and a piece that has hard, chewy kernels dispersed throughout the entire cob, which one would you pick? Not a very hard choice, when you look at it like that, is it? It's really common sense.

3. And, finally, we generally become like those we follow. Just as our children imitate us, so we tend to imitate those who we follow and look up to. It's so important that we choose any human we follow so very carefully.

———

I don't know how many of my favorite pastors, teachers, and authors are going to compromise going forward. It's a little unnerving, quite frankly. But, whoever I choose to follow, my first and foremost loyalty must be to the Lord and His Word and never to a person.

And I encourage you to do the same. Please do this even with what I have written here. *My opinions mean nothing.* Please, please run all you read here through the grid of the Word. I am honored that you have chosen to read this book, but I never want you to value my word over the Word of God.

If we are going to discern properly, we need to stop blindly following those who would lead us over the spiritual cliff. We need to immerse ourselves in the Word of God and examine everything that comes our way for the red flags of compromise. Our spiritual health–and the spiritual health of those we disciple (including our own kids and grandkids!)–is dependent upon this.

Reawakening
the Conscience

This chapter may be hard to read for some of you. It's about a topic that most people would prefer to ignore. But I believe it is something that can't be ignored if we truly desire to learn to discern. I am referring to the role that worldliness plays in deadening our consciences.

Let me explain. Sometimes I wonder how so many who call themselves Christians cannot see what is going on within the church. How can they not understand how ravenous wolves (posing as sheep) are changing the very mission and purpose of the church from within?

I believe it's because many of them have so deadened their consciences, that they aren't even willing (or able?) to call sin *sin*. Not only can they not tell the difference between true and false, but they are starting to fudge and rationalize about the differences between right and wrong. And when we lose our ability to discern right from wrong, our ability to discern what is true from the false has already left us.

You may be asking: *How does worldly entertainment affect my discernment?* I have an answer for that and any thinking person will have to admit these are true. Worldly entertainment changes us in the following ways–

1. It keeps us from our Bibles. While this may not be true 100% of the time, it is certainly often true. How many times have you heard someone say that don't have time to read the Word but they will somehow have had time to watch TV?

2. It keeps us immersed in the goings-on of the world. When we think of worldly entertainment, we often think of the bad things, but I would submit to you that even the news and sports can steal our affections if we aren't careful. While these things aren't bad in and of themselves (most of the time), they will keep us immersed in the culture and, instead of separating from the world (as we are told to do in **James 1:27** and **James 4:4**) we become fascinated by it.

3. It changes our values and hardens our hearts. I can't tell you how many people have told me they can watch anything they want on TV because they know right from wrong and it doesn't affect them. That they can listen to worldly music espousing sex, drugs, and alcohol because they aren't going to ever do those things. Besides a stance like that begging the question why any believer would desire such entertainment (why would we, as a believer, want to fill our lives with the things God has clearly said He *hates*? **Galatians 5:19-21**), it also does have to be acknowledged that these things *do* change our values. They make us less sensitive to sin and harden our hearts.

4. It makes us more susceptible to desiring the world's approval. When we become immersed in the world the approval of the world can be all-consuming. When we love the world, we want to be loved by the world. But this, carried out to its fullest, will keep us from salvation. In John 12, this very thing happened. Here we are told that some of the Pharisees believed Jesus but they so feared man's opinion, rather than God's, that they refused to act on that belief. **John 12:43** simply puts it like this: *for they loved the glory that comes from man more than the glory that comes from God.* **When we fill our minds with the world, we become much less interested in truth and much more interested in popularity.**

5. It keeps us from caring about what matters in life. Entertainment is meant to entertain. Its goal is to distract us from real life for a little while and give us some refreshment. It is not a bad thing, in and of itself. But we have become so enthralled with being entertained that we are distracted from our real lives much of the time. With our smart phones, our tablets, and things like *Netflix* and *YouTube*, we are constantly *entertained*. Many of us can't even stand in a line at a grocery store or sit at a booth in a restaurant without pulling out our phones. This has exponentially compounded our interest in the trivial, while eliminating interest in the serious stuff of life at the same time. How many Christians do you know who ever discuss God? Or heaven and hell? Or the Bible? When serious matters do arise, most arguments are based on popular opinion rather than the Word of God. I believe this is in much part due to our obsession with entertainment.

So why do I say this? What proof do I have? Let me share three different testimonies regarding this–

First, I want to share something my brother, Pastor Dean, has shared with me. Shortly after college, he made two decisions. He stopped watching football on Sunday afternoons and instead read the Word. And, second, he removed all rock music from his life (including Christian rock). He credits these two decisions with changing his life completely. He says it was like withdrawing from a drug (if you have ever tried to give up rock music, you will find that it is extremely addictive) but that it was a life-changing decision. These two decisions not only strengthened His walk with the Savior, but also deepened his love for the Word and his hatred for the world.

Second, I want to share my own testimony. Mine is a little more like one of those jagged lines that goes up and down and all over the place. While I have always been conscious that worldly entertainment has great potential for evil in my life, I have not always been as careful as I ought. And I have had stages in my life where it has drawn me into its snare. But God has really been working on me and I am so grateful to say that, over the past fifteen years or so, God has removed much of my desire for worldly entertainment and I am totally changed as a Christian because of this.

And, **third**, I want to share the testimonies of two of my children. Both have told me this at two separate times. But let me back up a bit. When my kids became teenagers, we loosened up our standards a bit. Oh, not near so much as most of their friends, but we didn't want them to look like complete losers and not be aware of anything in the world and so we caved. At that time, we allowed secular rock into our home, as long as it didn't have "bad lyrics". We regret that choice. Even if one song of a particular artist doesn't have bad lyrics, the others probably do. And, to add to that, the artists' lifestyles are rarely anything we want modeled. About five years ago or so, I just started pleading with God that my children would love righteousness and hate evil. And He has answered this prayer in incredible ways! One of those ways was that two of my children decided—on their own—to eliminate secular music from their lives. And both have told me (in two separate conversations, without the other one's knowledge) what a difference this has made in their own discernment and spiritual walk with God.

You have to know this: What we fill our minds with does affect our discernment. But there is good news! We can reawaken our consciences! It is not too late. If we start eliminating or drastically reducing (in the case of things like news and sports) the world's entertainment and filling our minds with the Word of God, we will find our consciences will get back to work, informing and enlightening us about not only what is right and wrong, but also about what is true and false.

Okay, so now I have given you several ways our conscience is affected by worldly entertainment and I have given you three real life examples of how this has happened. As you read, you probably found yourself in one of four places and I'd like to speak to all four.

First, you may be one of those who doesn't really have strong feelings about entertainment. You may like to watch a show or two, but you aren't addicted. You may have a pop station on in your car but it's just there. I would like to encourage you to continue to purify your life and to deepen your desire to please your Savior and to worry less about being "cool" in the eyes of the world.

Second, you may be one who is truly addicted to *Netflix* binges or your smartphone or to rock music. You realize you should change but you just don't really want to. You enjoy your addiction and to change it now seems completely overwhelming. I want to suggest to you that you start praying that God would give you the desire to change.

Or perhaps you already desire to change and you want to start now but you don't even know where to begin. Pray for strength and guidance. You cannot do this alone.

God is faithful and He will answer these prayers! I know this because He answered my prayers when I called out to Him about the music that was in my life. I loved it so much and I didn't know how I could ever give it up. But He not only helped me stop listening to it, He completely removed the desire for it. This happened years ago and it still feels like a miracle!

Third, you may be someone who thinks I am completely crazy. This chapter makes even make you a bit angry and you honestly believe that I am wrong. If you are one of these, then I ask you–I beg you—to go to God's Word to research what I am saying. Turn away from the viewpoints of popular authors or speakers and turn to the Word of God before you make your final determination.

And, **fourth**, you may agree with me. You may have witnessed this dynamic in your own life. I would ask those of you in this group to share this unpopular message with your family and friends as the Lord gives you opportunity. So many of us Christians love the world. And this love is stunting our growth and keeping us from discerning. It is removing our effectiveness as a witness for Christ and it is making us so vulnerable to wolves who are invading the church in droves now. If you see this and you believe it, please don't be afraid to say it. This is the time to be brave and speak up!

May we continue to conform to the image of Christ through the word of God, rather than being conformed to this world as we endeavor to learn to discern.

Living in the Light

The other day I heard a popular Christian contemporary song. As I really paid attention to the familiar words for the first time, it dawned on me that one of the lines was clearly unbiblical. When I pointed it out to the friend who sat beside me, she laughed and remarked that I find something wrong with everything.

Hmmm…

Is that true?

Is that what I have become? Am I really someone who is looking for things to be heretical or false? Always looking for the worst? Honestly, I had to do a little soul-searching. This is certainly not what I want people to think about me. And yet…

When we learn to discern, we end up being caught between the proverbial rock and hard place. When we start understanding just how far away the culture and the mainstream church are moving from biblical truth, the agenda behind it, and with what lightning speed it's happening then the heresies, the compromises, and the ungodly alliances become so obvious. It becomes like second nature to spot it. This naturally leads to some questions and problems.

Yesterday we had a wonderful day of warm sunshine after several gloomy, damp days. The sunshine made the whole world look so much brighter. The grass looked greener and the birds sang louder. Sunshine changes everything.

When we start understanding what is going on in the world and particularly within the church, it can cast a very dark shadow on our whole lives. Just like the cloudy day dims our physical world, so, too, can discernment dim our spirit–if we allow it to.

So, as we learn to discern, we must answer this question:

Since we are now living in marvelous light (I Peter 2:9), how do we keep what we are learning from casting a dark shadow on our friendships, our families, our churches, and on our own personal world?

Stated another way: *How can we make sure that the light in us isn't engulfed by the negativity of what is going on around us?*

It can affect so much if not handled correctly. Practically speaking, it can cause us to be depressed (if we don't take our thoughts captive); it can cause rifts between friends and family (if we never stop talking about it); and it can develop a habit in us to start being critical about everything (even things that aren't biblical).

I think we can all agree that no one wants to be around a depressed, critical person who constantly talks about how the world is ending. So how can we be effective discerners, deepening our understanding of what's going on in the world, while keeping our eyes and hearts focused on the Lord? There is a balance that needs to be found and God's Word can help us to find it. Let's look at eight specific things we learn there.

1. Always seek Christ first.

Matthew 6:33 *But seek first the kingdom of God and His righteousness, and all these things shall be added to you.*

Philippians 3:8 *Yet indeed I also count all things loss for the excellence of the knowledge of Christ Jesus my Lord, for whom I have suffered the loss of all things, and count them as rubbish, that I may gain Christ.*

Sometimes we can get so caught up in learning what is going on with the world's system or with Satan's agenda that we neglect our Bible Study. In fact, we may even fool ourselves into thinking that since we are studying about the church, this will suffice as our Bible Study. Oh, may this never be! It is far better to be in the Word and know absolutely nothing about what's going on in the world. For it is impossible to be godly and wise believers without the Word. It is impossible to even discern without the Word. We must seek God first, above all else. All studies–even studies of discernment–must come after this priority.

2. Remember that our citizenship is in heaven.

Philippians 3:23-24 *For our citizenship is in heaven, from which we also eagerly wait for the Savior, the Lord Jesus Christ, who will transform our lowly body that it may be conformed to His glorious body, according to the working by which He is able even to subdue all things to Himself.*

It is hard to become depressed or overly distressed about something that doesn't really affect our future one way or another. Imagine you are a temporary visitor to a foreign country that is experiencing some political upheaval. While you would naturally be somewhat interested in what's going on (especially as it may affect you getting home), you wouldn't grow too excited, because you know that you are leaving that country soon for your safe and secure home. And so, we, too, must remember that we are just temporarily passing through this world. We don't belong here. When we can remember this, it helps us to find perspective and helps to keep the shadows from descending.

3. Remember that very few Christians care about discernment like you do.

I Peter 3:8 *Finally, all of you be of one mind, having compassion for one another; love as brothers, be tenderhearted, be courteous;*

Sometimes we can get so caught up in what we are learning that it is all we think about. And then it may become all we talk about. But we must remember that most Christians simply do not care. They want to talk about other things. And while we must faithfully and gently warn and proclaim the truth as God gives us opportunities, we should never become so passionate about what we are learning that it becomes the only thing we talk about. May we always be kind and courteous and sensitive to the interest (or *disinterest*) of others as we learn to discern.

4. Our opinions must be based on scripture alone.

Acts 17:11 *These were more fair-minded than those in Thessalonica, in that they received the word with all readiness, and searched the Scriptures daily to find out whether these things were so.*

We must be so careful to make sure anything we say is based on God's Word alone. Unless it is in God's Word, it is not worth arguing over. We must pick our battles. Thankfully, by searching God's Word daily to know Him, to understand truth, and to become better discerners, we naturally become less critical of things that have nothing to do with biblical truth because we are also learning the importance of encouraging, edifying, and loving others, as well.

5. God is sovereign. He's got this.

Job 38:4a *Where were you when I laid the foundations of the earth?* (If you have time, read the whole chapter)

God is sovereign. Life in this beautiful world is not without organization and design. We are not a bunch of cells haphazardly thrown together. Every single thing that happens is a part of God's detailed and eternal plan. We can become a little panicky about the world and church's situation when we forget that God is sovereign over all that's going on.

6. Stop looking back.

Philippians 3:13-14 *Brethren, I do not count myself to have apprehended; but one thing I do, forgetting those things which are behind and reaching forward to those things which are ahead, I press toward the goal for the prize of the upward call of God in Christ Jesus.*

Oh, how discontent and sorrowful we can become if we keep remembering what used to be. And isn't this such a temptation? Especially for those of us who can remember better days. But we know that God has us right where we are for such a time as this. Referring back to point #5, His will and ways are utterly and absolutely sovereign. His plan includes you being right here right now. The past is past but we can make a difference for Him right now and in whatever time remains for us before His return. Let's stop looking back and start looking forward!

7. God Wins!

Revelation 19:6-8 *And I heard, as it were, the voice of a great multitude, as the sound of many waters and as the sound of mighty thunderings, saying, "Alleluia! For the Lord God Omnipotent reigns! Let us be glad and rejoice and give Him glory, for the marriage of the Lamb has come, and His wife has made herself ready." And to her it was granted to be arrayed in fine linen, clean and bright, for the fine linen is the righteous acts of the saints.*

As we see Satan wreaking havoc around us, may we never forget that he is going to lose. We know from reading Revelation that no matter how much Satan schemes and confuses and deceives, he is going to lose. No matter what battles he seems to be winning, he will lose the war. Isn't that so encouraging? Our God reigns!

8. God is faithful.

Lamentations 4:22-24 *Through the Lord's mercies we are not consumed, Because His compassions fail not.*
They are new every morning; Great is Your faithfulness.
"The Lord is my portion," says my soul,"Therefore I hope in Him!"

One of the things that can be a little scary as we learn to discern is the awareness of what it could possibly mean for our own well-being, and, of even more concern for most of us, the well-being of our children, grand-children, and even great-grandchildren.

We see dark, menacing storms on the future's horizon and we can grow fearful. And yet, God will not fail us. Thankfully, we have the testimonies of faithful Christians who have endured through the worst of times. We read the accounts of martyrs who have died singing and praising God while burning at the stake and they remind us: God will be faithful to the end. He will not take us where He will not strengthen us to go. We are His. No one can snatch us out of His hand and no one can touch us without His permission. This is such a comforting thought as we learn just how evil this world is.

As we learn to discern, may we remember that, while the world's horizon darkens, we can still be full of marvelous light because we know the King of Kings personally and He has promised to take care of us (I Peter 5:7).

Discerners often have a bad reputation. In fact, when we simply mention the word "discernment" these days, most professing Christians start rolling their eyes. While some of this is born out of the human tendency to love the world and the things of the world, I believe it is also because those that discern can tend to be the things I mentioned above: Negative, harsh, and thoughtless in their dealings with people; focused on the wrong thing; and critical about things that aren't even in the Bible.

May we not allow this in our own lives. May we not let what we are learning lead us to have a dark and mournful spirit. May we not be so passionate about discernment that we stop studying the scriptures. And may we be patient with believers who can't see, praying for them and offering kind and truthful answers when they ask questions. Let's be interested in all of life and not be consumed by an unhealthy desire to unearth all of the darkness in the world.

We Christians are to be the ones that are faithfully sharing our light for we have the <u>only true Hope</u>

available to mankind in this dark, dark world. Let's not get distracted. The blackness around us should make us shine brighter, not turn us into dim, flickering flames struggling to stay alight.

> *You are the light of the world. A city that is set on a hill cannot be hidden. Nor do they light a lamp and put it under a basket, but on a lampstand, and it gives light to all who are in the house. Let your light so shine before men, that they may see your good works and glorify your Father in heaven.*

Matthew 5:14-16

Knowing When to Speak Up

I was mindlessly moving a load of laundry from the washer to the dryer. My mind was on other things and I wasn't really paying attention to what I was doing. Without thinking, I grabbed a dime that was lying near the dryer's lint trap and tossed it in the trash.

Oops!

I looked at the trash and I pondered the worth of the dime. And then I turned back to my task. I simply did not find the dime to be valuable enough to warrant digging through the trashcan. This made me wonder about what amount of money would make digging in the trash worthwhile for me? A quarter? A dollar? At what point would I deem the amount valuable enough that it would propel me to work to get it back?

I think we need to consider this same principle when we are looking at discernment. A few years ago, there was a huge "to-do" in the discernment world. What I saw happening there was someone who was making a huge deal over a "dime". While I did agree with this person's point of view on the subject matter at hand, I did not see that it was worth a fight. A few other Christian leaders had the same opinion as me and ended up being maligned by this other man who thought everyone else should be making as big a deal over this "dime" as he was!

One of the hardest things we must learn to do as we grow in discernment is know when something is worth a confrontation. **Romans 12:18** teaches us that we are to be at peace with all men, as much as it depends on us. This is an important verse, giving us a framework in which we are to live all of life.

Unfortunately, this is not going to always be possible. We know from scripture that we are going to be hated by the world and that there will be many false teachers. This naturally means that we will have some run-ins, as we try to stand for the truth.

So, how exactly do we know if something is important enough to speak up about in our families, churches, or anywhere else?

Here are a few guidelines to follow–

1. The situation at hand is about God, His Word, and His glory.

This is, by far, the most important key in our determination if something is worth defending or contending for. It should never be about our pride, our reputation, our importance, and certainly should never be about our need to prove ourselves. Something that is worth standing up for will always be about God's glory and about protecting the truth of God's Word.

It is never about ME.

But this is quite the challenge, isn't it? Sometimes it is hard to discern if we are standing for God or for our own pride. We have this need to prove ourselves or to be "right" and we can get all entangled in our own selfish agenda–sometimes even when are standing up for the true and right thing! We must have humble hearts that are on the constant look-out for sins like pride, selfishness, and anger. We must regularly ask the Lord for a right heart and attitude and that He will fill us with His love and grace as we fight the good fight. *(I Timothy 6:12)*

2. It is morally wrong.

There are an abundance of verses expounding on the things that are an offense to our Holy God. We know that sexual immorality, lying, sorcery, anger, theft, pride etc. are always wrong and therefore should be something that those who claim to be Christians should avoid. (Check out these passages for more clarity and detail on the sins that God hates: *Exodus 20:1-17; Colossians 3:5-6; Galatians 5:19-21; 2 Timothy 3:1-7.)*

If we know God hates these things, then this should be our guideline of things we want to avoid in all aspects of our lives. This would include our entertainment (already addressed in chapter 11), something that believers mostly ignore now and, for some reason, seem to believe is irrelevant to the rest of their spiritual health.

As those who desire to follow God whole-heartedly, our desire should be to live a pure and holy life. God's Word clearly teaches that, as regenerated souls, we are to live transformed lives that are clearly different and separated from the world *(I Peter 1:15-16; Jude 1:20; Philippians 1:9-10; 2 Timothy 2:22; Romans 12:1-2; I Peter 2:9; Romans 13:13-14; Colossians 3:10).*

This is not a wildly popular thing to stand for. In fact, it is not even marginally popular. But we need to speak up because God's glory and reputation are damaged by those who live worldly, sinful lives while claiming to belong to Him.

3. Scripture is misinterpreted and twisted.

2 Thessalonians 2:15 tells us this: *So then, brothers, stand firm and hold to the traditions that you were taught by us, either by our spoken word or by our letter.*

Since scripture was written, there has been an accepted interpretation. Oh, there have been councils and meetings to discuss things, but God has miraculously protected the integrity of scripture throughout the millennia.

However, Satan is always trying to mess with it just enough that he will mislead people. He has done this throughout history, but I highly doubt it has ever been so much as right now.

When someone gives some wild, out-of-context interpretation of scripture it is time to stand up! When someone tries to rationalize worldliness, homosexuality, evolution, or any other ungodly sin or human philosophy, it is time to stand for the truth of God's Word. We cannot let our enemy win this battle, for this is the battle's core: *Is scripture 100% true, inerrant, and inspired, or isn't it?*

Because we know that scripture is all of these things--true, inerrant, and inspired--we must speak up when it's maligned.

Of course, the problem with this is that most of us do not have enough biblical knowledge to really provide a biblical defense. This is really why I write. I want to encourage you to know the Word so that you can live godly lives and contend for the faith.

Our goal should be to run every single thing through the grid of scripture. Our desire should be to approach what we find there with a humble heart willing to obey.

If we accept the Bible as it is written, literally, it all makes so much sense. And, even more amazing, the facts presented in science (I am talking about *facts* and not *theories*) and the historical record supports it all!

You will find it incredible and even miraculous when you give yourself to serious study of this amazing Book. But, so often, we don't know because we don't study. And– if I may be so bold–we don't study because other things take priority in our hearts and lives.

If you take one thing away from this book, I hope it will renew and strengthen your desire to study the Word. I hope that it will lead you to grasp not only the necessity of studying the Bible but also to understand the incredible reward and protection that is ours when we actually do it.

4. Christ's role is diminished.

Oh, how many false teachers diminish the role of Christ! If you are deciding whether something is worth the fight, ask yourself this: *How do they treat Christ?*

Do they turn His sacrifice on the cross into a mere event without supernatural ramifications? Do they teach that Christ is one of many ways to be reconciled to God? Do they teach that man is basically good and that Jesus is just a good example to follow? Do they teach that Christ is there to do one's bidding? Do they teach that Christ is simply a good teacher?

You will be surprised how even the most mainstream teachers and authors are teaching error in regards to Jesus Christ. And this is worth the fight!

Perhaps you don't feel like you really know Jesus like you should. May I encourage you to get to know Him in the way God has provided—through His perfect Word?

While Jesus is the theme of the whole Bible (yes, even the Old Testament!), you can start by reading the Gospels. This is a great place to get started in knowing your Savior and will help you to speak the truth about Him to those who have it so wrong.

5. Primary Christian Doctrines are compromised.

As believers, we do need to know doctrine (which may be contrary to what you have been told). Being unfamiliar with words like justification, sanctification, and glorification leaves you vulnerable to false teachers. Having at least a basic understanding of what the Bible teaches about (to name a few) the Trinity, God's Sovereignty, salvation, God the Father, Jesus Christ, the Holy Spirit, and about the Church will strengthen and prepare you for the vicious and unrelenting attacks that Satan wages against these doctrines.

I would add here that understanding what the Bible teaches us about the last days and about Israel are secondary issues but are still beneficial–and interesting– to study.

Finding a solid, biblical resource can be most helpful. I recommend Pastor Dean Good's series on biblical doctrine which can be found both at *Growing4Life* (on the page called *Know the Scriptures*) and on his church website (*gcno.org*).

6. Be socially wise.

Now, with the final two items on this list, we are moving from biblical compromise to having social discernment. If someone you barely know starts sharing about how much they love *The Shack* or *Jesus Calling,* don't start off on a long monologue on why they are not doctrinally sound books. Go ahead and say something casually and if they express interest, then, by all means, have a conversation. But don't confront acquaintances and strangers. They have absolutely no reason to listen to you. Gauge their interest and be wise. And, most importantly, pray for them.

7. Consider the spirit of the person with whom you are having a discussion.

We must evaluate the person we are speaking to and ask ourselves: *Is this person humble and teachable or are they closed and proud?* When we find ourselves in conversation with someone who thinks they know everything, who won't bend, who doesn't listen…then it's probably wisest to simply state our biblically-based concern while refusing to be drawn into argument or debate. Only the Holy Spirit can remove that blind pride. We could talk for forever and not move them an inch. In these cases, we must allow the Lord to use us to plant His seeds and to challenge them with some thoughts. We do not want to become a thorn in their side that pricks at every opportunity. This is not how we practice discernment.

The above is not an exhaustive list. Practicing biblical discernment is a challenge, particularly when it comes to sharing what we are learning. And there is little personal reward for speaking up.

I have mentioned this before and I will mention it again: *Most Christians simply do not want to hear the truth about their favorite authors and speakers.* And because they do not want to hear, they will view you as annoying or negative and they may ridicule you or express their frustration with what they will call your "negativity".

It is important that this not stop you from sharing the truth because we know that the truth of the Bible not only has the power to save us from our sins but also to protect us as we navigate this barren landscape we call "Christianity" in this day and age. The Truth will set us free!

Deception leads to lost souls. It's a terrible thing. True love speaks up! Let's keep our eyes focused on what is important and not get embroiled in our hurt feelings and relational skirmishes here on earth. May we pray steadfastly, study the Word faithfully, and be emboldened to speak when God presents us with an opportunity.

What Is the Best Way to Share What I Am Learning?

As you have been learning to discern, you have been learning some pretty important lessons. Lessons such as the importance of looking below the surface of the appealing messages that mainstream Christianity promotes to see the anti-biblical messages that are *really* being taught. You have been learning to compare all you hear, read, and see to what the Bible says. And you are beginning to understand that not everyone who professes Christ is actually a true believer and that just because something is labeled "Christian" does not necessarily mean it is representing Jesus Christ. In fact, many speakers and authors are downright false teachers, coming as "angels of light" (2 Corinthians 11:14) to trick and deceive God's people.

So now what? Do we share what we are learning with others? Or do we just stay quiet?

I think it is clear in scripture that our job is to share the truth with others (Ephesians 4:14-15; Jude 3-4). This includes telling others about the love and grace of Jesus, as well as the not-so-popular topics of God's wrath, sin, and hell. And, yes, it also includes warning others of false teachers (Ephesians 5:11; Romans 16:17-18).

A natural question we may have as we contemplate these things is: *Do we wait for God to open a door or do we barge right through and speak up, even when we aren't asked?*

These are hard questions to answer, as each situation is so different. But I hope that this chapter may give you some helpful principles and insight as you start seeking to share the truths you are learning with others. Keep in mind that our conversations about discernment should be conducted with a humble heart and always based on God's Word.

<u>Principles for a Public Setting</u>

First, let's first consider our setting. How we bring up touchy topics in a private setting is going to be very different than how we do so in a public setting. Let's look at a few principles for a public platform when someone is praising a false teacher. How do we know if we should say something and, if we do feel compelled to do so, what is the best way to go about it?

1. Gravely consider your responsibility in the situation. Are you the teacher or leader of a Bible Study, a teacher or leader in a church, or a leader in an organization? In other words, are you responsible for the adherence to the truth of God's Word in the setting where the false teacher is being praised? If so, then you will be accountable to God for what is being taught. Say something but do so using the Bible to confirm what you are saying and speak with a soft voice and much grace. If someone has an issue or wants to argue, kindly ask them to discuss it with you privately afterwards.

If you are simply participating in the group or setting, it is often best to approach the teacher or leader afterwards with a clear passage of scripture, perhaps along with some outside facts that would be pertinent, and ask them to investigate. Each situation is different and each group is different, so it is best to judge these situations on a case-by-case basis.

2. Never belittle or ridicule the person you are talking to or about. If we feel compelled to speak up, we must never, ever belittle or minimize anyone personally. We must keep to the facts. And we must do all that's in our power to speak with great love, continually pointing people to God's Word, demonstrating how the teacher or movement does not agree with it. It is important to not get caught up in our own personal opinions, puffing ourselves up, acting like we have some special information that they just aren't "smart enough" to have.

Now, this can be challenging because sometimes people perceive us to be belittling someone when we really aren't. When we speak the truth, people often automatically feel criticized. And, in this current culture, disagreement has become synonymous with belittling and intolerance. We can't control this, but if we stick to the facts of someone's false ministry, comparing them to scripture, we are handling it correctly.

3. Use great discretion when posting and discussing on social media. Be sure to evaluate anything you share or post to be sure it is factual, scriptural, and loving and respectful in its tone. If someone wants to debate, end it quickly, indicating your willingness to discuss it privately, if they would so desire.

If a friend or family member has posted something positive about a false teacher, consider talking to them privately rather than commenting publicly. Social media platforms have made this an ugly, ugly world when it comes to debates and disagreements. While it is can be quite beneficial to use social media to share truth, we must be careful that it is never a place where we are viciously or pridefully stating the truth with no care about how we are hurting and crushing people in the process.

4. What about at my church? If there is a false teacher or a worldly system invading your church, first bathe the situation in prayer. Ask the Lord to open your pastor or elder's eyes. And then go respectfully to talk with leadership about what you see. Do not make a big public to-do over it and do not grab people to take your side. These responses are extremely damaging to the church.

The next inevitable question is: *But what if they don't listen? What if nothing changes?* It pains me to say this, but I have heard about, and personally heard from, so many who have been completely belittled and scorned by their pastors and leaders in their beloved churches for holding to the truth of God's Word. When they go to their leadership with a grave and valid concern that is backed by what scripture clearly teaches (perhaps about a false teacher that is being used for a Bible Study or a worldly, deceitful movement that is sneaking its way into the leadership's vision for the church) they are immediately shut down. They are told that this is what "leadership has decided" and that if they don't like it, they must move on. Sadly, this is the way most churches are doing ministry now. It truly is a travesty and totally opposed to what scripture teaches.

That being said, there may come a time that you may have to leave your church. Do not do this lightly. Dedicate much prayer and study the scriptures diligently to see if this issue (or issues) warrants leaving. Seek wise, godly counsel as you strive to do what's right regarding this very difficult decision.

Principles for a Private Setting

You will actually find that most of your interactions with people regarding discernment will be at a private level. They will take place in the halls of your church, over e-mail or the phone, or at dinner with friends.

How do we handle these conversations?

First, we need to determine if the person is—

• **Humble and interested**

• **Proud and closed**

OR

• **Apathetic and disinterested**

What kind of person are you talking to? There are a few questions you can ask yourself to quickly make this determination even as you are speaking to them—

1. Are they asking thoughtful questions?

2. Is their body language tense?

3. Are they listening to you as you speak?

4. Do they keep going back to their own opinions without any scripture?

5. Do they look bored?

If they are asking thoughtful questions, listening to your responses, and speaking kindly (even if you don't agree with their conclusions), then this is probably an *open, humble, and interested person*. This is someone with whom we can at least hold a conversation.

If they are not really considering what we are saying but are simply giving their own opinions without scripture to back them up; if they are speaking with anger and agitation; if they aren't listening at all; well, then they are *closed, proud, and uninterested.*

If they seem bored with the conversation; if they look away and seem to be distracted; if they keep checking their phone, then you are dealing with someone *who is apathetic and disinterested* in really knowing what is going on. There are many people who just would rather not know.

Almost everyone falls into one of these three groups. And you can quickly figure it out as you learn to understand the cues that people give. How we deal with the first group is very different than how we deal with the second two groups. Let's look at principles for both groups.

<u>Principles for Open, Humble, and Interested Individuals</u>

1. Don't overload them with information. If someone shows interest, our natural response is to gather all kinds of websites, articles, and videos to confirm what we are saying. However, an overwhelmed person is likely to grow discouraged and give up. Carefully choose one or two of your best resources to share and let them know you are willing to talk more if they are interested.

2. Encourage them to study scripture for themselves. When it comes right down to it, the insight and discernment to spot and recognize false teachers and false teaching comes from our study of the Word. We are helpless and must lean on others if we are biblically illiterate. The MOST important thing, *by far*, that we can do is encourage them to study the Word!

3. Speak with a kind and level voice as you discuss these hard and ugly truths about the mainstream church and modern-day Christianity. These things–as we find them out–can (rightly so) make us angry. Those of us who tend to be more expressive can sound angry or aggressive without even realizing it. Practice talking about these things without being harsh, unkind, or loud.

4. Remember that it is God who works in the heart. Respect their space and submit to God's sovereignty in their lives as they sort through things. Sometimes all of this (as you may remember when you started learning the truth of what is going on in the mainstream church) can be extremely overwhelming and they simply need to take a step back. Give them the time they need to process. Life may have given them a curveball they weren't expecting and they just don't have time to think about it right now. Don't grow discouraged if they seem disinterested after that initial contact.

Instead, recognize that you have been given the privilege to plant a seed of truth and that God will use it however He sees fit. He might bring someone else along to water that seed or they may eventually come back to ask you a question. Some will never show any further interest. It is critical to recognize that we are simply soldiers for Christ, doing His bidding as He gives us opportunities. That is all that is required of us. We can count on Him to take care of the rest.

5. Pray for them. If someone seems really interested, pray and ask the Lord to open their eyes and give them insight from His Word. If you are concerned because you see someone continuing in false teaching–even after you have had some wonderful conversations with them and they seem to moving in the right direction, pray for them, as well. I can honestly say there are few things more discouraging than this but there is little else we can do, since harping or nagging them about it generally produces the opposite result of what we hope for, while also putting great strain on the relationship. God is faithful and He answers prayers like this. Remember, He doesn't need us. He blesses us by using us but He certainly doesn't need us to open someone's eyes to the truth.

Principles for the Closed, Proud OR Apathetic, and Uninterested

1. Don't push. Someone who doesn't want to know *just doesn't want to know*. You are not going to change them. Only God can do that.

2. Know when to stop talking. The Bible says that we shouldn't cast our pearls before swine (Matthew 7:6). I think this principle applies when we are speaking the truth of God's Word in this area of discernment. If the person you are talking to is disinterested or even hostile towards what you are saying, then it is time to stop talking. Sometimes we just need to discern that it's time to end the conversation.

3. Don't grow bitter or angry towards that person. These conversations can quickly turn ugly and can fill us with a deep and abiding grudge if we don't go to the Lord, asking Him to help us forgive. These situations can become even more trying when the person, frustrated with our biblical message, spreads lies about us or does everything possible to hinder our ministry. It is in these times that we must make a choice to forgive and move on. If not, our ministry most certainly will be hindered!

4. Pray. And then pray some more. No heart is too hard. We know this from scripture (Paul is a great example of this!) We must pray with faith, remembering that God can change the hardest of hearts.

Above are a few principles that I hope you will find helpful as you navigate this unpopular path of Christian discernment. I wish I could say that I have always followed these myself, but, alas, I am still learning, just like you. But let's keep having the conversations. It is critically important that we keep shining a light into the darkness of the worldly church. If you mess up, evaluate what you could have done or said differently and keep going. Don't let your failures keep you from speaking up.

Unfortunately, there will often be fall-out. There are some who just don't want to hear the truth and just the fact that you have said something has turned them into your enemy. We can't control this. But we can control how we treat people after a conversation that is less than what we hoped for. And again, I mention **Romans**

12:18. The principle in this verse cannot be overstated as we consider this topic of sharing with others–

If it is possible, as much as depends on you, live peaceably with all men.

This verse tells us that it is not always possible to live peaceably with everyone, but it also makes it clear that we must do whatever we can to do so. This means forgiving (no grudges allowed!) and treating someone kindly and lovingly, no matter how a conversation went.

Thankfully, you will also find that there are a few who will "get it". They are the ones who grasp what is going on and the grave significance of it. You will find that talking with them and encouraging them is a great joy.

I have been thinking a great deal recently about how we really are now on a rescue mission. The current situation is an inferno on a massive scale and we are not stopping it. But we can turn people to God's Word and share what we have learned as God gives us opportunity. Let's not be swayed by a church and culture that tells us that speaking truth is an unloving thing to do. It is, in fact, one of the most loving things we *can* do.

God bless you as you share His truth with those He puts in your path.

When You Need a Little Help

Sometimes we know that something is off with an author but we just can't put our finger on it. Something is most definitely wrong…but what is it? What do we do?

We must judge all we come across by the Word of God. Acts 17:11, I Thessalonians 5:20-21, and I John 4:1 make it clear that God expects us to do this. But often we don't know the Word of God well enough ourselves and we need a little help to discern if that new teacher is someone we can trust or that latest trend is something we can join.

Someone asked me recently if I could share some of the trusted resources I use to help me to discern. But I keep running into a big problem: Christian platforms, websites, and celebrities are compromising at an unprecedented level. I feel uncomfortable even recommending any because my trust has been eroded so often.

Because I can't go back and remove a recommendation in this book near as easily as I could remove one from my website, I am not going to give any specific recommendations here but, rather, I would like to give you principles and guidelines as you do your own research on false teachers—

1. ALWAYS be a Berean, even with a trusted site or author. As we have seen over the past few years, teachers, authors, and websites are falling for false doctrine and/or joining with false teachers at record speed. It's a little surreal, actually. All that to say: A site you have trusted for years that has a great track record may very well leave the straight and narrow path of biblical Christianity. Always keep your eyes and ears open and never trust blindly. The days of blind trust are over. (But perhaps there never really were any…? That's probably how Christianity got to this place to begin with!)

2. Remember that some discernment sites can be rather unkind and harsh. While I don't condone this kind of attitude and I generally try to avoid these sites, the tone of a post or article does not change whether something is true or not. *Always look for truth.* Whether it is cloaked in love or not doesn't change whether or not it is true. I have tried not to recommend this kind of site, but as you do your own research you may find this kind of site. Let your guiding principle for a site be its clear examination of a teaching as compared to scripture.

3. Avoid sites that are "witch hunts" or centered around personal attacks. While naming names is not a sin (we see Paul do this several times in scripture), it should not be done lightly. We are called to compare a teacher's doctrine to scripture and to examine their lifestyle in the light of the Word. We are not called to tear them apart with abundant criticism and to create our own personal vendetta against them. Watch out for sites and authors that do this and avoid them completely.

4. Keep learning the Bible more and more, so that it becomes natural to discern on your own. You will find out that as you do this, you will need other resources less and less. When we study the Bible with a spirit of submission and obedience to all it says (even the parts you don't like!), we will find that it will enable us to more quickly spot the deadly philosophies that are slithering into our homes and churches.

5. Never let discernment become our all-encompassing focus. All too often, people get so caught up in research that they let their Bible study dwindle. Our power for the Christian life lies in knowing the Word. Discernment is not a bad thing, but if it overtakes our life and becomes all we focus on, it has been used by Satan to distract us from what is most important. Be careful not to let that happen.

I hope these principles (and this entire book) will be a blessing to you as you strive to discern in this age of abundant heresies and unprecedented apostasy.

I leave you with these words from God's Word—

*But evil men and impostors will grow worse
and worse, deceiving and being deceived. But you
must continue in the things which you have learned
and been assured of, knowing from whom you have
learned them, and that from childhood you have known
the Holy Scriptures, which are able to make you wise
for salvation through faith which is in Christ Jesus.*

2 Timothy 3:13-15

www.ingramcontent.com/pod-product-compliance
Lightning Source LLC
Chambersburg PA
CBHW070907160726
48004CB00003B/1276